ESSENTIAL ELEMENTS

FOR BAND

COMPREHENSIVE BAND METHOD

TIM LAUTZENHEISER   **JOHN HIGGINS**   **CHARLES MENGHINI**
PAUL LAVENDER   **TOM C. RHODES**   **DON BIERSCHENK**

Band is… **M**aking music with a family of lifelong friends.
Understanding how commitment and dedication lead to success.
Sharing the joy and rewards of working together.
Individuals who develop self-confidence.
Creativity—expressing yourself in a universal language.
Band is… **MUSIC!**

Strike up the band,
Tim Lautzenheiser

HISTORY OF THE TRUMPET

The origins of the trumpet can be traced to ancient Egypt, Africa and Greece. These "natural" valveless trumpets were made of wood, bronze or silver. In the Middle Ages (500–1430), these instruments played only lower notes. During the Renaissance era (1430–1600), they performed at many ceremonial functions. Gradually, players began to develop their higher range, especially in the Baroque era (1600–1750).

Heinrich Stölzel introduced a valve trumpet in Berlin in 1814. By 1830, the B♭ Cornet was introduced in Europe. Valves made it possible to play all the notes of a chromatic scale on these two closely-related instruments.

Cornets and trumpets are the highest pitched members of the brass family. As one of the primary instruments in the sound of concert bands and jazz ensembles, they play melodies, harmonies and solos. A trumpet is longer than the more conically shaped cornet. In this book, we refer to the B♭ Trumpet, but the instructions apply to both instruments.

Virtually all important composers have written music for the trumpet, including J.S. Bach and W.A. Mozart. Some famous performers are Maurice André, Adolph Herseth, Doc Severinsen and Wynton Marsalis.

To create an account, visit:
www.essentialelementsinteractive.com

Student Activation Code
E1TP-0354-2766-7089

ISBN 978-0-634-00320-2
Copyright © 2004 by HAL LEONARD CORPORATION
International Copyright Secured   All Rights Reserved

HAL•LEONARD® CORPORATION
7777 W. BLUEMOUND RD. P.O. BOX 13819 MILWAUKEE, WI 53213

THE BASICS

Posture

Sit on the edge of your chair, and always keep your:
- Spine straight and tall
- Shoulders back and relaxed
- Feet flat on the floor

Breathing & Airstream

Breathing is a natural thing we all do constantly. To discover the correct airstream to play your instrument:
- Place the palm of your hand near your mouth.
- Inhale deeply through the corners of your mouth, keeping your shoulders steady. Your waist should expand like a balloon.
- Slowly whisper "tah" as you gradually exhale air into your palm.

The air you feel is the airstream. It produces sound through the instrument. Your tongue is like a faucet or valve that releases the airstream.

Producing The Essential Tone

"Buzzing" through the mouthpiece produces your tone. The buzz is a fast vibration in the center of your lips. Your embouchure (ahm´-bah-shure) is your mouth's position on the mouthpiece of the instrument. A good embouchure takes time and effort, so carefully follow these steps for success:

BUZZING
- Moisten your lips.
- Bring your lips together as if saying the letter "m."
- Relax your jaw to separate your upper and lower teeth.
- Form a slightly puckered smile to firm the corners of your mouth.
- Direct a full airstream through the center of your lips, creating a buzz.
- Buzz frequently without your mouthpiece.

MOUTHPIECE PLACEMENT
- Form your "buzzing" embouchure.
- Center the mouthpiece on your lips. Your teacher may suggest a slightly different mouthpiece placement.
- Take a full breath through the corners of your mouth.
- Start your buzz with the syllable "tah." Buzz through the center of your lips keeping a steady, even buzz. Your lips provide a cushion for the mouthpiece.

Taking Care Of Your Instrument

Before putting your instrument back in its case after playing, do the following:
- Use the water key to empty water from the instrument. Blow air through it.
- Remove the mouthpiece. Once a week, wash the mouthpiece with warm tap water. Dry thoroughly.
- Wipe off the instrument with a clean soft cloth. Return the instrument to its case.

Trumpet valves occasionally need oiling. To oil your trumpet valves:
- Unscrew the valve at the top of the casing.
- Lift the valve half-way out of the casing.
- Apply a few drops of special brass valve oil to the exposed valve.
- Carefully return the valve to its casing. When properly inserted, the top of the valve should easily screw back into place.

Be sure to grease the slides regularly. Your director will recommend special slide grease and valve oil, and will help you apply them when necessary.

MOUTHPIECE WORKOUT

Using only the mouthpiece, form your embouchure carefully. Take a deep breath without raising your shoulders. Begin buzzing your lips by whispering "tah" and gradually exhale your full airstream. Strive for an even tone.

"tah"

REST

"tah"

REST

valves

1   2   3

mouthpiece receiver

mouthpiece

hook

valve casings

first valve slide

second valve slide

third valve slide

water key

third valve slide ring

Getting It Together

Throughout this book, all instructions apply to both cornets and trumpets because they are played exactly the same way.

Step 1 Put your left thumb and fingers around the valve casings and pick up the trumpet. Your left hand supports the weight of the instrument.

Step 2 Place your left ring finger inside the ring of the third valve slide.

Step 3 Hold the mouthpiece at the wide end with your right hand. Gently twist the mouthpiece into the mouthpiece receiver.

Step 4 Arch your right hand to form a backwards "C." Place your thumb between the first and second valve casings. Place your little finger on top of the hook.

Step 5 Always sit or stand tall when playing. Hold the trumpet as shown:

READING MUSIC   Identify and draw each of these symbols:

Music Staff

The **music staff** has 5 lines and 4 spaces where notes and rests are written.

Ledger Lines

Ledger lines extend the music staff. Notes on ledger lines can be above or below the staff.

Measures & Bar Lines

Measure   *Measure*

Bar Line   *Bar Line*   *Bar Line*

Bar lines divide the music staff into **measures**.

Long Tone

To begin, we'll use a special "Long Tone" note. Hold the tone until your teacher tells you to rest. Practice long tones each day to develop your sound.

1. THE FIRST NOTE

Hold each long tone until your teacher tells you to rest.

G
○○○
1 2 3

"G" is played with **open valves**. Just rest your fingers lightly on the valves.

The Beat

The **beat** is the pulse of music, and like your heartbeat it should remain very steady. Counting aloud and foot-tapping help us maintain a steady beat. Tap your foot **down** on each number and **up** on each "&."

One beat = 1 &
           ↓ ↑

Notes And Rests

Notes tell us how high or low to play by their placement on a line or space of the music staff, and how long to play by their shape. **Rests** tell us to count silent beats.

♩ Quarter Note = 1 beat

𝄽 Quarter Rest = 1 silent beat

2. COUNT AND PLAY

Count: 1 & 2 & 3 & 4 &   1 & 2 & 3 & 4 &   1 & 2 & 3 & 4 &   1 & 2 & 3 & 4 &
Tap: ↓ ↑ ↓ ↑ ↓ ↑ ↓ ↑   ↓ ↑ ↓ ↑ ↓ ↑ ↓ ↑   ↓ ↑ ↓ ↑ ↓ ↑ ↓ ↑   ↓ ↑ ↓ ↑ ↓ ↑ ↓ ↑

3. A NEW NOTE

Look for the fingering diagram under each new note.

F
●○○

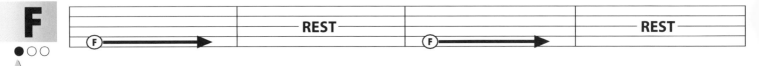

The black circles tell you which valves to push down. "F" is played with **1st valve**.

4. TWO'S A TEAM

Count & Tap: 1 & 2 & 3 & 4 &   1 & 2 & 3 & 4 &   1 & 2 & 3 & 4 &   1 & 2 & 3 & 4 &

5. HEADING DOWN

Practice long tones on each new note.

E
●●○

6. MOVING ON UP

Count & Tap: 1 & 2 & 3 & 4 &   1 & 2 & 3 & 4 &   1 & 2 & 3 & 4 &   1 & 2 & 3 & 4 &

Double Bar	indicates the end of a piece of music.	Repeat Sign	Without stopping, play once again from the beginning.

7. THE LONG HAUL

Double Bar ∨

8. FOUR BY FOUR

Repeat Sign ∨

Count & Tap: 1 & 2 & 3 & 4 &   1 & 2 & 3 & 4 &   1 & 2 & 3 & 4 &   1 & 2 & 3 & 4 &

9. TOUCHDOWN

10. THE FAB FIVE

1 & 2 & 3 & 4 &   1 & 2 & 3 & 4 &   1 & 2 & 3 & 4 &   1 & 2 & 3 & 4 &

Treble Clef
(G Clef) indicates the position of note names on a music staff: Second line is G.

Time Signature
indicates how many beats per measure and what kind of note gets one beat.

4 = **4 beats** per measure
4 = **Quarter** note gets one beat

Note Names
Each note is on a line or space of the staff. These note names are indicated by the Treble Clef.

THEORY

Sharp ♯ raises the note and remains in effect for the entire measure.

Flat ♭ lowers the note and remains in effect for the entire measure.

Natural ♮ cancels a flat (♭) or sharp (♯) and remains in effect for the entire measure.

11. READING THE NOTES *Compare this to exercise 10, THE FAB FIVE.*

1 & 2 & 3 & 4 &   1 & 2 & 3 & 4 &   1 & 2 & 3 & 4 &   1 & 2 & 3 & 4 &

12. FIRST FLIGHT

e e b b c c c   b b f f   e d c

13. ESSENTIAL ELEMENTS QUIZ *Fill in the remaining note names before playing.*

C D E

6

Notes In Review

Memorize the fingerings for the notes you've learned:

14. ROLLING ALONG

Go to the next line.

Double Bar

Half Note

♩ ──→ = 2 Beats

1 & 2 &

Half Rest

= 2 Silent Beats

1 & 2 &

15. RHYTHM RAP   *Clap the rhythm while counting and tapping.*

Clap

Repeat Sign

1 & 2 & 3 & 4 &   1 & 2 & 3 & 4 &   1 & 2 & 3 & 4 &   1 & 2 & 3 & 4 &   1 & 2 & 3 & 4 &   1 & 2 & 3 & 4 &

16. THE HALF COUNTS

1 & 2 & 3 & 4 &   1 & 2 & 3 & 4 &   1 & 2 & 3 & 4 &   1 & 2 & 3 & 4 &   1 & 2 & 3 & 4 &   1 & 2 & 3 & 4 &

17. HOT CROSS BUNS   *Try this song on your mouthpiece only. Then play it on your instrument.*

Breath Mark   ,   Take a deep breath through your mouth after you play a full-length note.

18. GO TELL AUNT RHODIE

American Folk Song

19. ESSENTIAL ELEMENTS QUIZ   *Using the note names and rhythms below, draw your notes on the staff before playing.*

F   G   F   E   F   E   D   C   D   E   F   E   F

Whole Note

○ ——→ = 4 Beats

1 & 2 & 3 & 4 &

Whole Rest

▬ = A Whole Measure of Silent Beats

1 & 2 & 3 & 4 &

Whole Rest hangs from a staff line.

Half Rest sits on a staff line.

20. RHYTHM RAP *Clap the rhythm while counting and tapping.*

21. THE WHOLE THING

Duet A composition with two different parts, played together.

22. SPLIT DECISION – Duet

Key Signature The **Key Signature** tells us which notes to play with sharps (♯) or flats (♭) throughout the music. Your Key Signature indicates the *Key of C* (no sharps or flats).

THEORY

23. MARCH STEPS

24. LISTEN TO OUR SECTIONS

25. LIGHTLY ROW

26. ESSENTIAL ELEMENTS QUIZ *Draw in the bar lines before you play.*

| **Fermata** | 𝄐 | Hold the note (or rest) longer than normal. |

27. REACHING HIGHER – New Note

Practice long tones on each new note.

Fermata

28. AU CLAIRE DE LA LUNE

French Folk Song

29. REMIX

THEORY

Harmony   Two or more notes played together. Each combination forms a *chord*.

30. LONDON BRIDGE – Duet

English Folk Song

HISTORY

Austrian composer **Wolfgang Amadeus Mozart** (1756–1791) was a child prodigy who started playing professionally at age six, and lived during the time of the American Revolution. Mozart's music is melodic and imaginative. He wrote more than 600 compositions during his short life, including a piano piece based on the famous song, "Twinkle, Twinkle, Little Star."

31. A MOZART MELODY

Adaptation

32. ESSENTIAL ELEMENTS QUIZ

Draw these symbols where they belong and write in the note names before you play:

9

33. DEEP POCKETS – New Note

34. DOODLE ALL DAY

35. JUMP ROPE

Pick-Up Notes

One or more notes that come before the first *full* measure. The beats of Pick-Up Notes are subtracted from the last measure.

36. A-TISKET, A-TASKET

Dynamics

f – *forte* (play loudly) mf – *mezzo forte* (play moderately loud) p – *piano* (play softly)

Remember to use full breath support to control your tone at all dynamic levels.

37. LOUD AND SOFT

38. JINGLE BELLS   *Also practice new music on your mouthpiece only.*   J. S. Pierpont

39. MY DREYDL   *Use full breath support at all dynamic levels.*   Traditional Hanukkah Song

Eighth Notes

Each Eighth Note = ½ Beat
2 Eighth Notes = 1 Beat
Play on down and up taps.

1 & 2 &

Two or more Eighth Notes have a *beam* across the stems.

▼ *Beam*

40. RHYTHM RAP *Clap the rhythm while counting and tapping.*

41. EIGHTH NOTE JAM

42. SKIP TO MY LOU

American Folk Song

43. LONG, LONG AGO *Good posture improves your sound. Always sit straight and tall.*

44. OH, SUSANNA

Stephen Collins Foster

HISTORY

Italian composer **Gioacchino Rossini** (1792–1868) began composing as a teenager and was very proficient on the piano, viola and horn. He wrote "William Tell" at age 37 as the last of his forty operas, and its familiar theme is still heard today on radio and television.

45. ESSENTIAL ELEMENTS QUIZ — WILLIAM TELL

Gioacchino Rossini

2/4 Time Signature

= **2 beats** per measure
= **Quarter** note gets one beat

Conducting

Practice conducting this two-beat pattern.

46. RHYTHM RAP

47. TWO BY TWO

Tempo Markings

Tempo is the speed of music. Tempo markings are usually written above the staff, in Italian.

Allegro – Fast tempo   **Moderato** – Medium tempo   **Andante** – Slower walking tempo

48. HIGH SCHOOL CADETS – March

John Philip Sousa

49. HEY, HO! NOBODY'S HOME – New Note

Dynamics

Crescendo (gradually louder)   *Decrescendo* or *Diminuendo* (gradually softer)

50. CLAP THE DYNAMICS

51. PLAY THE DYNAMICS

PERFORMANCE SPOTLIGHT

52. PERFORMANCE WARM-UPS

53. AURA LEE – Duet or Band Arrangement

(Part A = Melody, Part B = Harmony)

George R. Poulton

54. FRÈRE JACQUES – Round   *(When group A reaches ②, group B begins at ①)*

French Folk Song

PERFORMANCE SPOTLIGHT

55. WHEN THE SAINTS GO MARCHING IN – Band Arrangement

Arr. by John Higgins

56. OLD MACDONALD HAD A BAND – Section Feature

57. ODE TO JOY (from Symphony No. 9)

Ludwig van Beethoven
Arr. by John Higgins

58. HARD ROCK BLUES – Encore

John Higgins

Tie	A curved line connecting notes of the same pitch. Play one note for the combined counts of the tied notes.	= 2 Beats

59. FIT TO BE TIED

2 beats △

60. ALOUETTE

French-Canadian Folk Song

3 beats △

Dotted Half Note

 = 3 Beats

1 & 2 & 3 &

 ◄ Dot

A dot adds half the value of the note.

2 beats + 1 beat = 3 beats

61. ALOUETTE – THE SEQUEL

French-Canadian Folk Song

HISTORY American composer **Stephen Collins Foster** (1826–1864) was born near Pittsburgh, PA. He has become the most recognized song writer of his time for works such as "Oh Susanna," which became popular during the California Gold Rush of 1849. Among his most well-known songs are "My Old Kentucky Home" and "Camptown Races."

62. CAMPTOWN RACES

Stephen Collins Foster

Allegro

mf

63. NEW DIRECTIONS

64. THE NOBLES *Always use a full airstream. Keep fingers on top of the valves, arched naturally.*

3 beats △

65. ESSENTIAL ELEMENTS QUIZ

THEORY

$\frac{3}{4}$ Time Signature

$\frac{3}{4}$ = **3 beats** per measure
= **Quarter** note gets one beat

Conducting

Practice conducting this three-beat pattern.

66. RHYTHM RAP

Clap

1 & 2 & 3 & 1 & 2 & 3 & 1 & 2 & 3 & 1 & 2 & 3 & 1 & 2 & 3 & 1 & 2 & 3 & 1 & 2 & 3 & 1 & 2 & 3 &

67. THREE BEAT JAM

1 & 2 & 3 & 1 & 2 & 3 & 1 & 2 & 3 & 1 & 2 & 3 & 1 & 2 & 3 & 1 & 2 & 3 & 1 & 2 & 3 & 1 & 2 & 3 &

68. BARCAROLLE

Jacques Offenbach

Moderato

mf

HISTORY

Norwegian composer **Edvard Grieg** (1843–1907) wrote *Peer Gynt Suite* for a play by Henrik Ibsen in 1875, the year before the telephone was invented by Alexander Graham Bell. "Morning" is a melody from *Peer Gynt Suite*. Music used in plays, or in films and television, is called **incidental music**.

69. MORNING (from Peer Gynt)

Edvard Grieg

Andante

p   *mf*   *p*

Accent

Emphasize the note.

70. ACCENT YOUR TALENT

Clap

HISTORY

Latin American music has its roots in the African, Native American, Spanish and Portuguese cultures. This diverse music features lively accompaniments by drums and other percussion instruments such as maracas and claves. Music from Latin America continues to influence jazz, classical and popular styles of music. "Chiapanecas" is a popular children's dance and game song.

71. MEXICAN CLAPPING SONG ("Chiapanecas")

Latin American Folk Song

f

72. ESSENTIAL CREATIVITY

Compose your own music for measures 3 and 4 using this rhythm:

16

THEORY

Accidental

Any sharp, flat or natural sign which appears in the music without being in the key signature is called an **accidental**.

Flat ♭

A **flat** sign lowers the pitch of a note by a half-step. The note B-flat sounds a half-step below B, and all B's become B-flats for the rest of the measure where they occur.

73. HOT MUFFINS – New Note

△ Bb

△ Flat applies to all B's in measure.

74. COSSACK DANCE

75. BASIC BLUES – New Note

Flat applies to all B's in measure.

THEORY

New Key Signature

This Key Signature indicates the *Key of F* – play all B's as B-flats.

1st & 2nd Endings

Play through the 1st Ending. Then play the repeated section of music, **skipping** the 1st Ending and playing the 2nd Ending.

76. HIGH FLYING

2nd time

HISTORY

Japanese folk music actually has its origins in ancient China. "Sakura, Sakura" was performed on instruments such as the **koto**, a 13-string instrument that is more than 4000 years old, and the **shakuhachi** or bamboo flute. The unique sound of this ancient Japanese melody results from the pentatonic (or five-note) sequence used in this tonal system.

77. SAKURA, SAKURA – Band Arrangement

Japanese Folk Song
Arr. by John Higgins

17

78. **UP ON A HOUSETOP**

79. **JOLLY OLD ST. NICK – Duet**

See page 9 for additional holiday music, MY DREYDL and JINGLE BELLS.

80. **THE BIG AIRSTREAM – New Note**

81. **WALTZ THEME (THE MERRY WIDOW WALTZ)**

Franz Lehar

82. **AIR TIME**

83. **DOWN BY THE STATION**

84. **ESSENTIAL ELEMENTS QUIZ**

85. **ESSENTIAL CREATIVITY** *Using these notes, improvise your own rhythms:*

DAILY WARM-UPS

WORK-OUTS FOR TONE & TECHNIQUE

86. TONE BUILDER *Use a steady stream of air.*

87. RHYTHM BUILDER

88. TECHNIQUE TRAX

89. CHORALE *(Adapted from Cantata 147)* — Johann Sebastian Bach

THEORY

Theme and Variations

A musical form featuring a **theme**, or primary melody, followed by **variations**, or altered versions of the theme.

90. VARIATIONS ON A FAMILIAR THEME

Theme · Variation 1 · Variation 2

D.C. al Fine

At the **D.C. al Fine** play again from the beginning, stopping at **Fine** *(fee'- nay)*.
D.C. is the abbreviation for **Da Capo**, or "to the beginning," and **Fine** means "the end."

91. BANANA BOAT SONG

Caribbean Folk Song

Moderato · Fine · D.C. al Fine

Sharp   ♯

A **sharp** sign raises the pitch of a note by a half-step. The note F-sharp sounds a half-step above F, and all F's become F-sharps for the rest of the measure where they occur.

92. RAZOR'S EDGE – New Note

93. THE MUSIC BOX

Moderato

African-American spirituals originated in the 1700's, midway through the period of slavery in the United States. One of the largest categories of true American folk music, these primarily religious songs were sung and passed on for generations without being written down. The first collection of spirituals was published in 1867, four years after The Emancipation Proclamation was signed into law.

HISTORY

94. EZEKIEL SAW THE WHEEL

African-American Spiritual

Allegro

Slur

A curved line which connects notes of different pitch. Tongue only the first note in a **slur**.

95. SMOOTH OPERATOR

△ *Slur 2 notes – tongue only the first.*

96. GLIDING ALONG

△ *Slur 4 notes – tongue only the first.*

Ragtime is an American music style that was popular from the 1890's until the time of World War I. This early form of jazz brought fame to pianists like "Jelly Roll" Morton and Scott Joplin, who wrote "The Entertainer" and "Maple Leaf Rag." Surprisingly, the style was incorporated into some orchestral music by Igor Stravinsky and Claude Debussy. The trombones now learn to play a *glissando,* a technique used in ragtime and other styles of music.

HISTORY

97. TROMBONE RAG

Allegro

98. ESSENTIAL ELEMENTS QUIZ

Andante   Fine   D.C. al Fine

99. TAKE THE LEAD – New Note

Phrase

A musical "sentence" which is often 2 or 4 measures long. Try to play a **phrase** in one breath.

100. THE COLD WIND

101. PHRASEOLOGY
Write in the breath mark(s) between the phrases.

New Key Signature

This **Key Signature** indicates the *Key of G* – play all F's as F-sharps.

Multiple Measure Rest

The number above the staff tells you how many full measures to rest. Count each measure of rest in sequence:

1-2-3-4   **2**-2-3-4

102. SATIN LATIN

German composer **Johann Sebastian Bach** (1685–1750) was part of a large family of famous musicians and became the most recognized composer of the Baroque era. Beginning as a choir member, Bach soon became an organist, a teacher, and a prolific composer, writing more than 600 masterworks. This *Minuet,* or dance in 3/4 time, was written as a teaching piece for use with an early form of the piano.

103. MINUET – Duet

Johann Sebastian Bach

104. ESSENTIAL CREATIVITY
This melody can be played in 3/4 or 4/4. Pencil in either time signature, draw the bar lines and play. Now erase the bar lines and try the other time signature. Do the phrases sound different?

Natural ♮ A **natural** sign cancels a flat (♭) or sharp (♯) and remains in effect for the entire measure.

105. NATURALLY

Austrian composer **Franz Peter Schubert** (1797–1828) lived a shorter life than any other great composer, but he created an incredible amount of music: more than 600 art-songs (concert music for voice and accompaniment), ten symphonies, chamber music, operas, choral works and piano pieces. His "March Militaire" was originally a piano duet.

106. MARCH MILITAIRE

Franz Schubert

107. THE FLAT ZONE – New Note

108. ON TOP OF OLD SMOKEY

American Folk Song

Boogie-woogie is a style of the **blues**, and it was first recorded by pianist Clarence "Pine Top" Smith in 1928, one year after Charles Lindbergh's solo flight across the Atlantic. A form of jazz, blues music features altered notes and is usually written in 12-measure verses, like "Bottom Bass Boogie."

109. BOTTOM BASS BOOGIE – Duet

PERFORMANCE SPOTLIGHT

Solo with Piano Accompaniment

You can perform this solo with or without a piano accompanist. Play it for the band, the school or your family. It is part of **Symphony No. 9 ("From The New World")** by Czech composer **Antonin Dvorák** (1841–1904). He wrote it while visiting America in 1893, and was inspired to include melodies from American folksongs and spirituals. This is the **Largo** (or "very slow tempo") theme.

118. THEME FROM "NEW WORLD SYMPHONY"

Antonin Dvorák

Piano Accompaniment

24

SPECIAL TRUMPET EXERCISE – Lip Slurs

Lip Slurs are notes that are slurred without changing valves. Brass players practice these to develop a stronger airstream and embouchure, and to increase range. Add this pattern to your daily Warm-Ups:

Great musicians give encouragement to fellow performers. On this page, clarinetists learn their instruments' upper register in the "Grenadilla Gorilla Jumps" (named after the grenadilla wood used to make clarinets). Brass players learn lip slurs, a new warm-up pattern. The success of your band depends on everyone's effort and encouragement.

119. GRENADILLA GORILLA JUMP No. 1

120. JUMPIN' UP AND DOWN

121. GRENADILLA GORILLA JUMP No. 2

122. JUMPIN' FOR JOY

123. GRENADILLA GORILLA JUMP No. 3

124. JUMPIN' JACKS

THEORY

Interval

The distance between two pitches is an **interval**. Starting with "1" on the lower note, count each line and space between the notes. The number of the higher note is the distance of the interval.

125. ESSENTIAL ELEMENTS QUIZ

Write in the numbers of the intervals, counting up from the lower notes.

Intervals: 2nd

126. GRENADILLA GORILLA JUMP No. 4

127. THREE IS THE COUNT

128. GRENADILLA GORILLA JUMP No. 5

129. TECHNIQUE TRAX

130. CROSSING OVER – New Note

Trio A **trio** is a composition with three parts played together. Practice this trio with two other players and listen for the 3-part harmony.

131. KUM BAH YAH – Trio *Always check the key signature.*

African Folk Song

26

138. EASY GORILLA JUMPS

139. TECHNIQUE TRAX *Always check the key signature.*

140. MORE TECHNIQUE TRAX

141. GERMAN FOLK SONG

142. THE SAINTS GO MARCHIN' AGAIN

James Black and Katherine Purvis

143. LOWLAND GORILLA WALK

144. SMOOTH SAILING

145. MORE GORILLA JUMPS

146. FULL COVERAGE

THEORY

Scale

A **scale** is a sequence of notes in ascending or descending order. Like a musical "ladder," each step is the next consecutive note in the key. This scale is in your Key of C (no sharps or flats), so the top and bottom notes are both C's. The interval between the C's is an octave.

147. CONCERT B♭ SCALE (Trumpet – C SCALE)

THEORY

Chord & Arpeggio

When two or more notes are played together, they form a **chord** or **harmony**. This C chord is built from the 1st, 3rd and 5th steps of the C scale. The 8th step is the same as the 1st, but it is an octave higher. An **arpeggio** is a "broken" chord whose notes are played individually.

148. IN HARMONY *Divide the notes of the chords between band members and play together. Does the arpeggio sound like a chord?*

149. SCALE AND ARPEGGIO

HISTORY

Austrian composer **Franz Josef Haydn** (1732–1809) wrote 104 symphonies. Many of these works had nicknames and included brilliant, unique effects for their time. His Symphony No. 94 was named "The Surprise Symphony" because the soft second movement included a sudden loud dynamic, intended to wake up an often sleepy audience. Pay special attention to dynamics when you play this famous theme.

150. THEME FROM "SURPRISE SYMPHONY"

Franz Josef Haydn

151. ESSENTIAL ELEMENTS QUIZ – THE STREETS OF LAREDO

American Folk Song

Write in the note names before you play.

PERFORMANCE SPOTLIGHT

152. SCHOOL SPIRIT – Band Arrangement

W.T. Purdy
Arr. by John Higgins

Soli

When playing music marked **Soli**, you are part of a group "solo" or group feature. Listen carefully in "Carnival of Venice," and name the instruments that play the Soli part at each indicated measure number.

153. CARNIVAL OF VENICE – Band Arrangement

Julius Benedict
Arr. by John Higgins

DAILY WARM-UPS

WORK-OUTS FOR TONE & TECHNIQUE

154. RANGE AND FLEXIBILITY BUILDER

155. TECHNIQUE TRAX

156. CHORALE

Johann Sebastian Bach

HISTORY

The traditional Hebrew melody "Hatikvah" has been Israel's national anthem since the nation's inception. At the Declaration of State in 1948, it was sung by the gathered assembly during the opening ceremony and played by members of the Palestine Symphony Orchestra at its conclusion.

157. HATIKVAH

Israeli National Anthem

Eighth Note & Eighth Rest

♪ = 1/2 beat of sound
♪ = 1/2 beat of silence

158. RHYTHM RAP

159. EIGHTH NOTE MARCH

160. MINUET

Johann Sebastian Bach

161. RHYTHM RAP

162. EIGHTH NOTES OFF THE BEAT

163. EIGHTH NOTE SCRAMBLE

164. ESSENTIAL ELEMENTS QUIZ

165. DANCING MELODY – New Note

166. EL CAPITAN

John Philip Sousa

Reproduced by Permission of Boosey & Hawkes Music Publishers Ltd.

167. O CANADA

Calixa Lavallee,
l'Hon. Judge Routhier
and Justice R.S. Weir

168. ESSENTIAL ELEMENTS QUIZ – METER MANIA   *Count and clap before playing. Can you conduct this?*

Enharmonics

Two notes that are written differently, but sound the same (and played with the same fingering) are called **enharmonics**. Your fingering chart on pages 46–47 shows the fingerings for the enharmonic notes on your instrument.

On a piano keyboard, each black key is both a flat and a sharp:

169. SNAKE CHARMER

Enharmonic notes use the same fingering.

170. DARK SHADOWS

171. CLOSE ENCOUNTERS

Enharmonic notes use the same fingering.

172. MARCH SLAV

Peter Illyich Tchaikovsky

173. NOTES IN DISGUISE

Chromatic Notes

Chromatic notes are altered with sharps, flats and natural signs which are not in the key signature. The smallest distance between two notes is a half-step, and a scale made up of consecutive half-steps is called a **chromatic scale**.

174. HALF-STEPPIN'

French composer **Camille Saint-Saëns** (1835–1921) wrote music for virtually every medium: operas, suites, symphonies and chamber works. The "Egyptian Dance" is one of the main themes from his famous opera *Samson et Delilah*. The opera was written in the same year that Thomas Edison invented the phonograph—1877.

175. EGYPTIAN DANCE *Watch for enharmonics.*

Camille Saint-Saëns

176. SILVER MOON BOAT

Chinese Folk Song

German composer **Ludwig van Beethoven** (1770–1827) is considered to be one of the world's greatest composers, despite becoming completely deaf in 1802. Although he could not hear his music the way we can, he could "hear" it in his mind. As a testament to his greatness, his Symphony No. 9 (p. 13) was performed as the finale to the ceremony celebrating the reunification of Germany in 1990. This is the theme from his Symphony No. 7, second movement.

177. THEME FROM SYMPHONY NO. 7 – Duet

Ludwig van Beethoven

Russian composer **Peter Illyich Tchaikovsky** (1840–1893) wrote six symphonies and hundreds of other works including *The Nutcracker* ballet. He was a master at writing brilliant settings of folk music, and his original melodies are among the most popular of all time. His *1812 Overture* and *Capriccio Italien* were both written in 1880, the year after Thomas Edison developed the practical electric light bulb.

178. CAPRICCIO ITALIEN *Always check the key signature.*

Peter Illyich Tchaikovsky

179. AMERICAN PATROL

F.W. Meacham

180. WAYFARING STRANGER

African-American Spiritual

181. ESSENTIAL ELEMENTS QUIZ – SCALE COUNTING CONQUEST

PERFORMANCE SPOTLIGHT

182. AMERICA THE BEAUTIFUL – Band Arrangement

Samuel A. Ward
Arr. by John Higgins

183. LA CUCARACHA – Band Arrangement

Latin American Folk Song
Arr. by John Higgins

PERFORMANCE SPOTLIGHT

184. THEME FROM 1812 OVERTURE – Band Arrangement

Peter Illyich Tchaikovsky
Arr. by John Higgins

PERFORMANCE SPOTLIGHT

Solo with Piano Accompaniment

Performing for an audience is an exciting part of being involved in music. This solo is based on *Symphony No. 1* by German composer **Johannes Brahms** (1833–1897). He completed his first symphony in 1876, the same year that the telephone was invented by Alexander Graham Bell. You and a piano accompanist can perform this for the band or at other school and community events.

185. THEME FROM SYMPHONY NO. 1 – Solo *(Concert E♭ version)*

Johannes Brahms
Arr. by John Higgins

DUETS

Here is an opportunity to get together with a friend and enjoy playing music. The other player does not have to play the same instrument as you. Try to exactly match each other's rhythm, pitch and tone quality. Eventually, it may begin to sound like the two parts are being played by one person! Later, try switching parts.

186. SWING LOW, SWEET CHARIOT – Duet

African-American Spiritual

187. LA BAMBA – Duet

Mexican Folk Song

RUBANK® SCALE AND ARPEGGIO STUDIES

TRUMPET KEY OF C (CONCERT B♭)

TRUMPET KEY OF F (CONCERT E♭) *In this key signature, play all B♭'s.*

RUBANK® SCALE AND ARPEGGIO STUDIES

TRUMPET KEY OF G (CONCERT F) *In this key signature, play all F#'s.*

RHYTHM STUDIES

RHYTHM STUDIES

CREATING MUSIC

Composition

Composition is the art of writing original music. A composer often begins by creating a melody made up of individual **phrases**, like short musical "sentences." Some melodies have phrases that seem to answer or respond to "question" phrases, as in Beethoven's *Ode To Joy*. Play this melody and listen to how phrases 2 and 4 give slightly different answers to the same question (phrases 1 and 3).

1. ODE TO JOY

Ludwig van Beethoven

2. Q. AND A. *Write your own "answer" phrases in this melody.*

3. PHRASE BUILDERS *Write 4 different phrases using the rhythms below each staff.*

4. YOU NAME IT: _____

Pick phrase A, B, C, or D from above, and write it as the "Question" for phrases 1 and 3 below. Then write 2 different "Answers" for phrases 2 and 4.

Improvisation

Improvisation is the art of freely creating your own melody *as you play*. Use these notes to play your own melody (Line A), to go with the accompaniment (Line B).

5. INSTANT MELODY

You can mark your progress through the book on this page. Fill in the stars as instructed by your band director.

ESSENTIAL
ELEMENTS

STAR ACHIEVER

NAME_____

1. Page 2–3, The Basics
2. Page 5, EE Quiz, No. 13
3. Page 6, EE Quiz, No. 19
4. Page 7, EE Quiz, No. 26
5. Page 8, EE Quiz, No. 32
6. Page 10, EE Quiz, No. 45
7. Page 12–13, Performance Spotlight
8. Page 14, EE Quiz, No. 65
9. Page 15, Essential Creativity, No. 72
10. Page 17, EE Quiz, No. 84
11. Page 17, Essential Creativity, No. 85
12. Page 19, EE Quiz, No. 98
13. Page 20, Essential Creativity, No. 104
14. Page 21, No. 109

15. Page 22, EE Quiz, No. 117
16. Page 23, Performance Spotlight
17. Page 24, EE Quiz, No. 125
18. Page 26, Essential Creativity, No. 137
19. Page 28, No. 149
20. Page 28, EE Quiz, No. 151
21. Page 29, Performance Spotlight
22. Page 31, EE Quiz, No. 164
23. Page 32, EE Quiz, No. 168
24. Page 33, No. 174
25. Page 35, EE Quiz, No. 181
26. Page 36, Performance Spotlight
27. Page 37, Performance Spotlight
28. Page 38, Performance Spotlight

MUSIC — AN ESSENTIAL ELEMENT OF LIFE

FINGERING CHART

Bb TRUMPET/Bb CORNET

Instrument Care Reminders

Before putting your instrument back in its case after playing, do the following:

- Use the water key to empty water from the instrument. Blow air through it.
- Remove the mouthpiece. Once a week, wash the mouthpiece with warm tap water. Dry thoroughly.
- Wipe off the instrument with a clean soft cloth. Return the instrument to its case.

Trumpet valves occasionally need oiling. To oil your trumpet valves:

- Unscrew the valve at the top of the casing.
- Lift the valve half-way out of the casing.
- Apply a few drops of special brass valve oil to the exposed valve.
- Carefully return the valve to its casing. When properly inserted, the top of the valve should easily screw back into place.

Be sure to grease the slides regularly. Your director will recommend special slide grease and valve oil, and will help you apply them when necessary.

CAUTION: If a slide, a valve or your mouthpiece becomes stuck, ask for help from your band director or music dealer. Special tools should be used to prevent damage to your instrument.

Bb TRUMPET

Bb CORNET

○ = Open
● = Pressed down

Instruments courtesy of Yamaha Corporation of America, Band and Orchestral Division

FINGERING CHART

B♭ TRUMPET/B♭ CORNET

D

D♯ E♭

E

F

F♯ G♭

G

G♯ A♭

A

A♯ B♭

B

C

C♯ D♭

D

D♯ E♭

E

F

F♯ G♭

G

G♯ A♭

A

A♯ B♭

B

C

REFERENCE INDEX

Definitions (pg.)

Accent   15
Accidental   16
Allegro   11
Andante   11
Arpeggio   28
Bass Clef   5   *(Bass clef inst.)*
Bar Lines   3
Beat   4
Blues   21
Breath Mark   6
Chord   28
Chromatic Notes   33
Chromatic Scale   33
Common Time   26
Crescendo   11
D.C. al Fine   18
Decrescendo   11
Diminuendo   11
Dotted Half Note   14
Dotted Quarter Note   22
Double Bar   5
Duet   7
Dynamics   9
Eighth Note   10
Eighth Rest   31
Embouchure   2   *(Brass & WW's)*
Enharmonics   33
Fermata   8
1st & 2nd Endings   16
Flat   5
Forte (*f*)   9
Glissando   19   *(Trombone)*
Half Note   6
Half-step   33
Harmony   8
Interval   24
Key Signature   7
Largo   23
Ledger Lines   3
Measure   3
Mezzo Forte (*mf*)   9
Moderato   11
Multiple Measure Rest   20
Music Staff   3
Natural Sign   5
Notes   4
Phrase   20
Piano (*p*)   9
Pick-Up Notes   9
Quarter Note   4
Ragtime   19
Repeat Sign   5, 26
Rests   4, 6, 7, 31
Round (Canon)   12
Scale   28
Sharp   5

Slur   19
Soli   29
Solo   23, 38
Tempo   11
Theme And Variations   18
Tie   14
Time Signature   5
Treble Clef   5   *(Treble clef inst.)*
Trio   25
Whole Note   7

Composers

JOHANN SEBASTIAN BACH
• Chorale (from Cantata 147)   18
• Chorale   30
• Minuet   20
• Minuet   31
LUDWIG VAN BEETHOVEN
• Ode To Joy (from Sym. No. 9)   13
• Theme From Symphony No. 7   34
JOHANNES BRAHMS
• Theme From Sym. No. 1   38
  (Brass & Low WW's)
ANTONIN DVORÁK
• Theme From "New World Sym."   23
STEPHEN COLLINS FOSTER
• Camptown Races   14
• Oh, Susanna   10
EDVARD GRIEG
• Morning (from Peer Gynt)   15
FRANZ JOSEF HAYDN
• Theme From "Surprise Symphony"   28
FRANZ LEHAR
• Waltz Theme   17
WOLFGANG AMADEUS MOZART
• A Mozart Melody   8
• Eine Kleine Nachtmusik   38
  (High WW's)
JACQUES OFFENBACH
• Barcarolle   15
GIOACCHINO ROSSINI
• William Tell   10
CAMILLE SAINT-SAËNS
• Egyptian Dance   34
FRANZ SCHUBERT
• March Militaire   21
JEAN SIBELIUS
• Finlandia   26
JOHN PHILIP SOUSA
• El Capitan   32
• High School Cadets   11
PETER ILLYICH TCHAIKOVSKY
• Capriccio Italien   35
• March Slav   33
• 1812 Overture   37

World Music

AFRICAN
• Kum Bah Yah   25
AMERICAN
• American Patrol   35
• America The Beautiful   36
• Aura Lee   12
• Ezekiel Saw The Wheel   19
• Go Tell Aunt Rhodie   6
• Michael Row The Boat Ashore   26
• On Top Of Old Smokey   21
• Skip To My Lou   10
• Swing Low, Sweet Chariot   39
• The Streets Of Laredo   28
• Wayfaring Stranger   35
• When The Saints Go Marching In   13, 27
AUSTRALIAN
• Botany Bay   26
AUSTRIAN
• Austrian Waltz   26
CANADIAN
• Alouette   14
• O Canada   32
CARIBBEAN
• Banana Boat Song   18
CHINESE
• Silver Moon Boat   34
ENGLISH
• London Bridge   8
• Scarborough Fair   22
• Sea Chanty   22
FRENCH
• Au Claire De La Lune   8
• Frère Jacques   12
GERMAN
• German Folk Song   27
ISRAELI
• Hatikva   30
ITALIAN
• Carnival Of Venice   29
JAPANESE
• Sakura, Sakura   16
MEXICAN
• Chiapanecas   15
• La Bamba   39
• La Cucaracha   36
SCOTTISH
• Auld Lang Syne   22
TRADITIONAL HOLIDAY MUSIC
• Jingle Bells   9
• Jolly Old St. Nick   17
• My Dreydl   9
• Up On A Housetop   17